Help Me! Guide to Android for Seniors

By Charles Hughes

Table of Contents

West Bend Public Library
630 Poplar Street
West Bend, WI 53095
262-335-5151
www.west-bendlibrary.org/

Introduction to Android

Table of Contents

1. Turning the Device On or Off

When you first take your Android device out of the box, you will need to turn it on to use it (unless a store salesman already turned it on for you). To turn on most Android devices, you will need to locate the **Power** button. On almost all Android phones, this button is located either on the top or right-hand side of the phone, and is always marked with a ⏻ or ⏼ icon either on the button or right next to it. The button may be located on the back of some tablets.

There is rarely a need to turn your Android device off, since you can always silence it. If you do need to turn off your phone, such as when flying, you can press and hold the **Power** button on most phones, and then touch **Power Off** or **Turn Off**. You can turn off your Android tablet in the same manner.

2. Charging the Device

Every Android phone or tablet comes with a charging cable, which you can use to charge the battery when it is running low. Most Android devices will indicate that the battery is low with a message alert or when the battery icon at the top of the screen turns red.

To charge your Android device, plug one end of the cable into a power outlet, and plug the other end into your phone or tablet. Although its location varies, every Android device has a charging port that looks like this: ⬭ . This is where you need plug in the charging cable. The Android device will usually make a sound or vibrate when it begins to charge. If you do not hear a sound or feel a vibration, try checking the battery icon at the top of the screen to see whether it has changed. Also make sure that you have plugged in both ends fully, as phone or tablet cases may sometimes interfere with charging cables.

3. Finding the Android Buttons

Although the locations of Android buttons vary, every device has the following buttons:

Power Button - Turns the phone on and off. Locks and unlocks the phone. An example of a power button is shown in **Figure 1**.

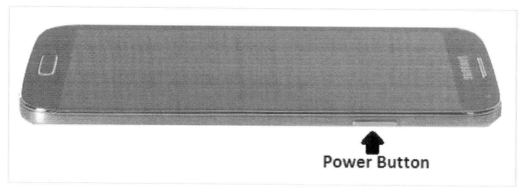

Figure 1: Power Button Example

Volume Control - Controls the volume of the ear piece, speaker phone, and music. An example of a Volume Control is shown in **Figure 2** (sometimes it will appear as two separate buttons next to each other on the side of the device).

Figure 2: Volume Control Example

Back Key - Returns the phone to the previous screen or menu. Sometimes, the Back key looks like this:

Menu Key - Opens a context menu, which gives you a list of options or settings based on the application that you are currently using. The Menu key is usually located on the front of the device near the bottom, or near the bottom of the screen itself. Newer models of Android phones and tablets do not have a Menu key.

Home Key- Displays the Home screen at any time. Sometimes, the Home key is a hard button, such as on Samsung's Galaxy S series. The Home key is also usually located on the front of the device near the bottom, or near the bottom of the screen itself.

4. Getting Around the Screens

Navigating the screens of your phone can be a challenge at first, but once you learn which gestures and buttons perform which functions, it will become easier with experience. Use the following tips to get around:

- Press the **Home** key or button to return to the Home screen at any time. The last viewed Home screen will appear. Press the **Home** button again to view the main Home screen. Any application or tool that is currently in use will be in the same state when it is re-opened.

- Slide your finger to the left or right to access additional Home screens from your main Home screen.

- When viewing a list of applications, move your finger up or down, or to the left or right to view more icons.

- Touch the ⬅ key at any time to return to the previous screen, menu, or application. Once you are at the main Home screen, the ⬅ button has no function.

- Touch the top of the screen and move your finger down to view all notifications.

5. Types of Objects on the Screen

Every screen on your Android contains one of three different types of objects:

- **Application Icon** - A computer program that opens in a new window, such as Email or a game. An application icon may look like the following on the screen: 📷. As shown here, even the camera is considered to be an application. Touch an Application icon to open that application.

- **Widget** - A tool that can be used directly from the Home screen without having to open it first like an application. Widgets usually take up the whole screen or a fraction of it, while applications are added as icons. For example, the Calendar widget is shown in **Figure 3**. If you touch a widget, the accompanying application usually opens. For example, on some devices, if you touch a day on the Calendar widget, the Calendar application opens showing the selected day.

- **Folder Icon** - A folder containing application icons. Please note that a folder cannot store widgets. When you touch a folder, it expands, showing the application icons that it contains. On some devices, you can organize application icons into folders by touching and holding an icon on the Home screen, and moving it on top of another icon.

Figure 3: Calendar Widget

6. Organizing Objects on the Screen

Every icon, widget, and folder on the screen can be moved around or deleted. You can also add new icons, widgets, and folders to the screen.

Adding a New Application Icon or Widget

To add an application icon or widget to a Home screen:

1. Touch the ▦ icon on the screen. The Apps screen appears. The appearance of the ▦ icon may be different, but it is usually in the lower right-hand corner of the screen.

2. Touch the screen and move your finger to the left or right to browse the applications and widgets that are installed on your phone or tablet. The application icons and widgets appear.

3. Touch and hold an application or widget icon. The Home screen appears. Do not release the screen.

4. Drag the icon to the desired location. If there is no room on the current screen, drag the icon to the left or right edge of the screen or on top of a Home screen thumbnail. The adjacent Home screen appears.

5. Release the screen. The application icon or widget is placed.

Moving an Application Icon or Widget

To move an application icon or widget, touch and hold it until your phone briefly vibrates or the icon stands out while the rest are partially darkened (most tablets do not vibrate). Drag your finger to the area where you would like to place the icon or widget. If you would like to move the icon or widget to another screen, hold it at the edge of the screen until the adjacent screen appears.

Deleting an Application Icon or Widget

To delete an application icon or widget from a Home screen:

1. Touch and hold an application icon or widget. The phone briefly vibrates or the icon stands out while the rest are partially darkened. 'Remove' or a Trash Can icon will appear at the top or bottom of the screen.

2. Drag the icon over 'Remove' or the Trash Can icon. The object may turn red.

3. Release the screen. The application icon or widget is deleted from the Home screen. Removing an application icon or widget from a Home screen does not delete the application or widget from your device.

Making Calls (Smartphones Only)

Table of Contents

1. Dialing a Number

Numbers that are not in your phonebook can be dialed on the keypad. To manually dial a phone number, touch the icon at the bottom of the screen. The appearance of this icon may vary, but will always have a phone receiver on it. The keypad appears. Enter a phone number and touch the button at the bottom of the screen. Similarly, this button may look different on your device, but will always have a phone receiver on it. The phone calls the number.

2. Calling a Contact

If a number is stored in your Phonebook, you may touch the name of a contact to dial it. Refer to *"Adding a New Contact"* on page 17 to learn how to add a contact to the Phonebook. To call a contact already stored in your Phonebook:

1. Touch the ![icon] icon at the bottom of the Home screen. The Phonebook appears. The appearance of this icon may vary based on your phone. Other examples of this icon include: ![icons]

2. Touch a contact's name. The Contact Information screen appears.

3. Touch the number that you wish to call. The phone dials the number.

3. Assigning a Speed Dial

If you have a specific contact that you call on a regular basis, you may assign the contact's number to a speed dial. This will allow you to press and hold a number on the phone keypad to quickly dial the number. To assign a speed dial:

1. Touch the ![icon] icon at the bottom of the screen. The keypad appears. The appearance of this icon may vary, but will always have a phone receiver on it.

2. Press or touch the ![menu] key. This is the menu key, and may also look like one of these: ![icons]

3. Touch **Speed dial**. The Speed Dial settings appear. If you do not see "Speed dial" in the menu, or if no menu appears, your phone may not support speed dialing.

4. Touch a Speed Dial number. The Address Book appears.

5. Touch the name of a contact. A list of phone numbers appears, if there is more than one assigned to the contact. The contact is assigned to the speed dial.

4. Returning a Recent Phone Call

After you miss a call, the phone will notify you of who called and at what time. The phone also shows a history of all recent calls. To view and return a missed call or redial a recently entered number:

1. Touch the ![icon] icon at the bottom of the screen. The keypad appears. The appearance of this icon may vary, but will always have a phone receiver on it.

2. Touch the ![icon] icon at the top of the screen. A list of recent calls appears. The appearance of this icon may vary based on your phone. Other examples of this icon include: ![icons]

3. Touch the name of a contact. The contact's information appears.

4. Touch a phone number. The phone dials the number.

5. Receiving a Voice Call

When receiving a voice call, the Incoming Call screen appears. To answer the call, touch the ![icon] icon and drag it to the right side of the screen. The call is connected. The appearance of this icon will vary, but will always look like a green phone. To decline the call, touch the ![icon] icon and drag it to the left side of the screen. The call is sent to voicemail. The appearance of this icon will also vary, but will always look like a red phone. On some phones, you just need to touch **Accept** or **Decline** when someone is calling you.

6. Using the Speakerphone during a Voice Call

All Android phones have a built-in Speakerphone, which is useful when calling from a car or when several people need to participate in a conversation. To use the Speakerphone during a phone call:

1. Place a phone call. The Calling Screen appears.

2. Touch the 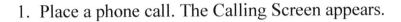 icon at the bottom of the screen. The speakerphone turns on. The appearance of this icon may vary based on your phone, but will always have the appearance of a small speaker.

3. Adjust the volume of the Speakerphone using the Volume Controls. Refer to *"Finding the Android Buttons"* on page 6 to locate the Volume Controls.

4. Touch the icon. The speakerphone turns off. The appearance of this icon may vary based on your phone, but will always have the appearance of a small speaker.

7. Using the Keypad during a Voice Call

You may wish to use the keypad while on a call in order to input numbers in an automated menu or to enter an account number. To use the keypad during a voice call, place the call and touch the icon. The keypad appears. The appearance of this icon may vary based on your phone. To hide the keypad, touch the icon. The appearance of this icon may vary based on your phone.

8. Using the Mute Function during a Voice Call

During a voice call, you may wish to mute your side of the conversation. When mute is turned on, the person on the other end of the line will not hear anything on your side. To use Mute during a call, place a voice call and touch the ⬚ icon at the bottom of the screen. The appearance of this icon may vary based on your phone. The phone mutes your voice and the caller(s) can no longer hear you, but you are still able to hear them. Touch the ⬚ icon. Mute is turned off. The appearance of this icon may vary based on your phone.

Managing Contacts

Table of Contents

---

1. Adding a New Contact

Android phones and tablets can store phone numbers, email addresses, and other contact information in their Phonebooks. To add a new contact to the Phonebook:

1. Touch the icon at the bottom of the screen. The Phonebook appears. The appearance of this icon may vary based on your phone. Other examples of this icon include:

2. Touch the icon at the top of the screen. This icon may also look like one of the following: . The New Contact screen appears. You may need to choose where you would like to save the contact first, either to your phone or to your Google account. Touch the desired option, if you see this screen.

3. Touch each field to edit it. Enter the contact's information in each field. You can also touch the ⊕ or ⊖ to add or remove a field, respectively.

4. Touch **Save** when you are finished. The contact's information is stored in the Phonebook.

2. Finding a Contact

After adding a contact to your phonebook, you may search for his or her information at any time. Not every phone or tablet has this feature. To find a stored contact:

1. Touch the 👤 icon at the bottom of the Home screen. The Phonebook appears. Other examples of this icon include:

2. Touch **Search** or **Find Contacts** at the top of the screen. The keyboard appears.

3. Start typing the name of the contact that you wish to find. The phone searches as you type, and the possible contact matches appear.

3. Editing Contact Information

After adding contacts to the Phonebook, you may edit their information at any time. To edit an existing contact's information:

1. Touch the 👤 icon. The Phonebook appears. Other examples of this icon include:

2. Touch the name of the contact that you wish to edit. The Contact Information screen appears.

3. Touch the ![icon] icon at the top of the screen. The Contact Editing screen appears. The appearance of this icon may vary, but will always look like a pencil.

4. Touch a field to edit it. Enter the contact's information into each field.

5. Touch **Save**. The contact's information is updated.

4. Deleting a Contact

You may delete a contact's information from the Phonebook in order to free up space or for organizational purposes. To delete unwanted contact information:

1. Touch the ![icon] icon. The Phonebook appears. Other examples of this icon include: ![icons]

2. Touch and hold the name of the contact that you wish to delete. The Contact Menu appears.

3. Touch **Delete**. A confirmation dialog appears.

4. Touch **OK**. The contact's information is deleted.

*Note: These instructions may vary based on the phone or tablet. On some devices, you may need to touch the contact's name, and then touch **Delete contact** or a trash can icon.*

5. Sharing a Contact's Information

When a contact is stored in the phonebook, all of the information for that contact can be shared. To share a contact's information:

1. Touch the icon. The phonebook appears. Other examples of this icon include:

2. Touch the contact's name. The Contact Information screen appears.

3. Touch and hold the name of the contact that you wish to share. The Contact Menu appears

4. Touch **Share namecard via** or **Share contact** to share the contact via text message. The Sharing Method menu appears.

5. Touch **Gmail** or **Text Message**, as these are the easiest ways to share contact information. A new message screen appears with the contact's information attached.

6. Enter the recipient's email address or phone number, and touch the button. The button used to send the message or email will vary depending on the device. Other examples of this icon may include an envelope with an arrow on it, such as: The contact's information is sent to the selected recipient.

6. Adding a Contact to Favorites

In order to find your most frequently used contacts more quickly, you may wish to add them to your Favorites. To add a contact to Favorites:

1. Touch the [icon] icon. The Phonebook appears. Other examples of this icon include: [icons]

2. Touch and hold the name of the contact. The Contact menu appears.

3. Touch **Add to favorites**. The contact is added to your Favorites.

Note: These instructions may vary based on the phone or tablet. On some devices, you may need to touch the contact's name, and then touch **Add to Favorites**, *or touch an icon in the shape of a star to add the contact to your Favorites.*

Text Messaging (Smartphones Only)

Table of Contents

1. Composing a New Text Message

The phone can send text messages to other mobile phones. To compose a new text message:

1. Touch the ![icon] icon at the bottom of the Home screen. The Messaging screen appears. The appearance of this icon may vary based on your phone. Other examples of this icon include: ![icons]

2. Touch the [icon] icon. The New Message screen appears. Other examples of this icon include: [icons]. On some phones, you simply need to touch **New Message**.

3. Type the name of a contact or enter a phone number. Suggestions appear while typing. The addressee or phone number is entered.

4. Touch **Enter message** and enter a message. Touch the [icon] button. The message is sent and appears as a conversation, sorted by send date. The button used to send the message will vary depending on the device. Other examples of this icon will usually include an envelope with an arrow on it. On some phones, you simply need to touch **Send**.

2. Copying, Cutting, and Pasting Text

The phone allows you to copy or cut text from one location and paste it to another. Copying leaves the text in its current location and allows you to paste it elsewhere. Cutting deletes the text from its current location and allows you to paste it elsewhere. To cut, copy, and paste text:

1. Touch and hold text on the screen. The Text options appear. To learn how to compose a message, refer to *"Composing a New Text Message"* on page 22.

2. Touch one of the following options to perform the associated action:

   - **Select All** - Selects all of the text in the field.

   - **Cut** - Removes the text while copying it to the clipboard. Touch and hold any text field, even in an outside application, and touch **Paste** to enter the cut text.

   - **Copy** - Leaves the text in the field while copying it to the clipboard. Touch and hold any text field, even in an outside application, and touch **Paste** to enter the copied text.

Note: The 'cut' and 'copy' options only become available when text is selected.

3. Using the Auto-Complete Feature

While entering a text message, some phones will automatically make suggestions to auto-complete words, which appear above the virtual keyboard. This is especially useful when a word is very long. To accept a suggestion, touch the word. The word is inserted into the current message.

4. Receiving Text Messages

Any Android phone can receive text messages from any other mobile phone. When receiving a text message, the phone vibrates once, plays a sound, or both, depending on the settings.

When you receive a text message, an envelope, such as this one ✉ will appear at the top of the screen. To open a newly received text message, touch the status bar at the top of the screen and drag it down (the bar where the time, battery, and signal bars are located). The Notifications screen appears. Touch the message with the ✉ icon next to it. The new text message opens.

5. Reading Text Messages

You may read any text messages that you have received, provided that you have not deleted them. To read stored text messages, touch the ✉ icon. The Messaging screen appears. Touch a conversation. The conversation opens. Other examples of this icon include:

6. Forwarding Text Messages

The forwarding feature on the phone allows a text message to be copied in full and sent to other recipients. To forward a text message:

1. Touch the icon. The Messaging screen appears. Other examples of this icon include:

2. Touch a conversation. The Conversation opens

3. Touch and hold a text message. The Message options appear.

4. Touch **Forward**. The New Message screen appears with the original message copied into the message field.

5. Enter a phone number or the name of a contact. The recipient is selected.

6. Touch the button. The text message is forwarded. The button used to send the message will vary depending on the device. Other examples of this icon will usually include an envelope with an arrow on it. On some phones, you simply need to touch **Send**.

7. Deleting Text Messages

You can delete separate text messages or an entire conversation, which is a series of text messages between you and one or more contacts.

Warning: Once deleted, text messages cannot be restored.

To delete an entire conversation:

1. Touch the icon. The Messaging screen appears. Other examples of this icon include:

2. Touch and hold a conversation. The Conversation menu appears.

3. Touch **Delete thread** or **Delete conversation** (or just **Delete**), depending on the phone. A Confirmation dialog appears.

4. Touch **OK**. The conversation is deleted.

To delete a separate text message:

1. Touch the icon. The Messaging screen appears. Other examples of this icon include:

2. Touch a conversation. The conversation opens.

3. Touch and hold a text message. The Message options appear.

4. Touch **Delete message**, or simply **Delete**, depending on the phone. A confirmation dialog appears.

5. Touch **OK**. The message is deleted.

8. Adding an Attachment to a Text Message

A picture or video can be attached to any text message. To send a text message with an attachment:

1. Refer to *"Composing a New Text Message"* on page 22 and follow steps 1-3.

2. Touch the icon to the right of the 'Enter message' field. The Attachment menu appears. The appearance of this icon may vary based on your phone, but will almost always look like a paper clip.

3. Click one of the following links to learn how to attach the associated media:

9. Attaching a Picture

Android phones can send media messages containing pictures. To attach a picture to a text message:

1. Refer to *"Adding an Attachment to a Text Message"* on page 26 and follow steps 1-3. The Attachment menu appears.

2. Follow the steps in the appropriate section below:

Taking and Attaching a Picture

1. Touch the [icon] icon. The camera turns on. The appearance of this icon may vary based on your phone, but will always look like a camera.

2. Touch the [button] button. The picture is captured and displayed on the screen for review. The appearance of this button may vary based on your phone, but will always be located at the top or bottom of the screen.

3. Touch **Discard** to retake the photo or touch **Save** to attach it to the text message. The photo is attached and the text message appears.

Attaching a Picture from a Photo Album

1. Touch the [icon] icon. The Gallery opens. Other examples of this icon include: [icons]

2. Touch the album that contains the photo that you wish to attach. The thumbnails of the photos in the album appear.

3. Touch a photo. A [check mark] mark appears next to the selected photo.

4. Touch **Done**. The photo is attached and the text message appears.

10. Attaching a Video

The phone can send media messages containing a video. To attach a video to a text message:

1. Refer to *"Adding an Attachment to a Text Message"* on page 26 and follow steps 1-3. The Attachment menu appears.

2. Touch the button. The camcorder turns on. The appearance of this icon may vary based on your phone, but will always look like a camcorder.

3. Touch the button. The video begins to record. The appearance of this button may vary based on your phone, but will always be located at the top or bottom of the screen.

4. Touch the button. The camcorder stops recording and the preview screen appears.

5. Touch **Discard** to retake the video or touch the icon in the center of the screen to preview it. The video plays.

6. Touch **Save**. The video is attached to the text message.

11. Saving Attachments from Text Messages

After receiving an attachment in a text message, it can be saved to your phone. To save an attachment from a text message:

1. Touch the ▨ icon. The Messaging screen appears. Other examples of this icon include: ▨ ▨ ▨ ▨

2. Touch a conversation. The conversation opens.

3. Touch and hold the attachment in the text message. The Message options appear.

4. Touch **Save attachment**. A list of files that are attached to the open conversation appears.

5. Touch an attachment to select it. A ✓ mark appears next to each selected attachment.

6. Touch **Save**. The attachment is saved to the Gallery.

Note: These instructions may vary depending on your phone. On some phones, simply touching the attachment without holding your finger down on the screen will allow you to save it.

Managing Pictures and Videos

Table of Contents

1. Taking a Picture

Every phone has a different camera. Here are a few facts about phone cameras:

- The cameras in newer phones allow you to take pictures and capture videos with much better quality.

- Some cameras allow you to zoom in by touching the screen with two fingers at the same time, and moving your fingers apart.

- Some phones have two cameras, one on the front and one on the back of the phone.

To take a picture, touch the icon. The appearance of this icon may vary based on your phone, but will always look like a camera. The camera turns on. Touch the icon to switch cameras, if your phone has two cameras. Touch the button. The picture is captured, and stored in the 'Camera' album. The appearance of this button may vary based on your phone, but will always be located at the top or bottom of the screen.

2. Capturing a Video

The phone has a built-in camcorder that allows you to capture videos. To capture a video:

1. Touch the icon. The camera turns on.

2. Touch the button. The camcorder begins to record video. The appearance of this icon may vary based on your phone, but will always look like a camcorder.

3. Touch the button at any time to pause the camcorder.

4. Touch the button. The camcorder stops recording, and the video is stored in the 'Camera' album.

3. Browsing Photos and Videos

You can browse pictures without activating the camera. To view saved images:

1. Touch the icon. The Gallery opens. Other examples of this icon include:

2. Touch an album. The album opens and the thumbnails of the photos in it appear.

3. Touch a photo or video. The photo appears in full-screen mode or the video begins to play.

4. Touch the screen and move your finger to the left or right. Other photos and videos in the same album appear.

5. Touch the button. The thumbnails of the pictures in the current album appear.

4. Starting a Slideshow

The phone can play slideshows using the pictures stored in the Gallery. To start a slideshow:

1. Touch the icon. The Gallery opens. Other examples of this icon include:

2. Touch an album. The album opens.

3. Touch the key or button. The Album menu appears.

4. Touch **Slideshow**. The slideshow begins. On some phones, you will have the opportunity to change some settings before starting the slideshow. You do not have to touch these.

5. Touch **Start**. The slideshow begins.

6. Touch the screen anywhere. The slideshow ends and the photo album appears.

Note: These instructions will vary based on your phone. Some phones may not have the slideshow feature.

5. Deleting Photos and Videos

Warning: Once a photo or video is deleted, there is no way to restore it, so make sure you do not want the selected files.

To free up some space in the phone's memory, try deleting photos or videos from the Gallery. To delete a photo or video:

1. Open a photo album. Refer to *"Browsing Photos and Videos"* on page 31 to learn how.

2. Touch and hold a photo or video. The photo is selected and a ✔ mark appears next to it.

3. Touch as many photos and videos as desired. The items are selected.

4. Touch the 🗑 icon. A confirmation dialog appears. The appearance of this icon will vary based on your phone, but will always look like a trash can. On some phones, you will need to simply touch **Delete**.

5. Touch **OK**. The selected items are deleted.

Using the Web Browser

Table of Contents

---

1. Navigating to a Web Page

You can surf the Web using your phone. To navigate to a Web page using a web address, or URL:

1. Touch the ![globe icon] icon, or touch the ![grid icon] icon and then touch the ![globe icon] icon. The Web browser opens. The appearance of the ![globe icon] icon will vary based on your device, but will usually look like a globe.

2. Touch the address bar at the top of the screen. The address bar will already have an address written in it when you touch it, and will appear as such: www.NAMEOFSITE.com, where "NAMEOFSITE" is the address of the current website. The address is highlighted and the virtual keyboard appears.

3. Enter the Web address (such as www.google.com), and touch **Go**. The device navigates to the corresponding website.

2. Adding and Viewing Bookmarks

Your device can store favorite web pages as bookmarks to allow you to access them faster in the future. To add a bookmark:

1. Navigate to a web page. Refer to *"Navigating to a Web Page"* on page 34 to learn how.

2. Touch the ▣ key. The Web browser menu appears.

3. Touch the ☆ icon, or touch **Add Bookmark**, depending on your device. The Add Bookmark screen appears.

4. Enter a name for the bookmark and touch **Save**. The web page is saved to your bookmarks.

To view saved bookmarks:

1. Touch the ☆ icon at the top of the page. On some devices, you may need to touch the ▣ key, and then touch **Bookmarks**. A list of bookmarks appears.

2. Touch a bookmark. The Web browser navigates to the web page.

3. Working with Links

In addition to touching a link to navigate to its destination, there are other link options. Touch and hold a link to see all link options. The following options are available:

- **Copy link address** - Copies the web address to the clipboard. Touch and hold an empty space in any application and touch **Paste** to paste the link. For instance, you may use this to share a link with someone via text message.

- **Copy link text** - Selects the text in the link to be copied to another location. You can also touch and hold any text on a Web page to achieve the same effect.

- **Save Link** - Downloads the web page to the phone. To view a list of downloads, touch the ⊞ icon at the bottom of the Home screen and then touch **Downloads**. The Downloads screen appears. Touch a web page in the list. The Web browser opens and navigates to the Web page.

4. Searching a Web Page for a Word or Phrase

While surfing the web, any page can be searched for a word or phrase. To perform a search on a web page:

1. Navigate to a web page. Refer to *"Navigating to a Web Page"* on page 34 to learn how.

2. Touch the ▭ key. The Browser menu appears.

3. Touch **Find in page** (or **Find on page** on some devices). A search field appears at the top of the screen.

4. Enter the search term or phrase. The matching results are highlighted on the web page as you type. Alternatively, 'No matches' appears at the top of the screen if no matches are found.

5. Touch the ⋀ or ⋁ arrow to select the previous or next matching result, respectively. The currently selected result is highlighted.

6. Touch the 🔍 key (or touch **Search** on some devices). The virtual keyboard is hidden so that you can review the search results.

5. Viewing the Browsing History

Your phone or tablet stores all recently visited web pages in a list called the Browsing History. To view the Browsing History while using the Web browser:

1. Touch the address bar at the top of the screen. The web address is highlighted in blue.

2. Touch the ☆ icon at the top of the screen. The Bookmarks page appears.

3. Touch **History** at the top of the screen. The Browsing History appears.

Note: The instructions for viewing the Browsing History may vary based on the phone or tablet that you are using.

Managing Email

Table of Contents

1. Setting Up Email

Before you can receive, send, and read email on your device, you need to add your account to it. The first time that you run the Email application (accessed by touching the icon, and then touching the @ icon, which will vary, but always appear as an envelope), you will be presented with the option to add an account. Enter your email address and password, and then touch **Next** or **Sign In** to add your email account.

Note: These instructions may vary depending on your phone or tablet.

2. Reading Email

You can read your email on the phone using the Email application. To read email:

1. Touch the @ icon on the Home screen or touch the ▦ icon and then touch the @ icon. The Email application opens and the Inbox appears.

2. Touch an email in the list. The email opens.

3. In some email applications, you can touch the screen and move your finger to the left or right to view the previous or next email, respectively. Otherwise, press the ⮌ key to return to the Inbox, and select another email to open it.

3. Sending an Email

Compose email directly from the phone using the Email application. To write an email while using the Email application:

1. Open the Inbox. Refer to *"Reading Email"* on page 39 to learn how.

2. Touch the ✉ icon. The Compose screen appears.

3. Start typing the name of a contact for whom you have a saved email address. A list of suggestions appears.

4. Touch the contact's name. The contact's email address is inserted. Alternatively, you may type an email from scratch in the 'To' field.

5. Touch **Subject** and enter an optional topic for the email. Touch the text field below the 'Subject' field, and enter a message. The subject and message are entered.

6. Touch the ➤ button, or touch **Send**, (depending on your device). The email is sent.

4. Replying to Emails

After receiving an email, you can reply to the sender of the email. To reply to an email:

1. Open the Inbox. Refer to *"Reading Email"* on page 39 to learn how.
2. Touch an email. The email opens.

3. Touch the ⬅ icon next to the sender's email address. A new email is generated with the sender's email address already entered in the 'To' field.

4. Enter a message and touch the ➤ button (or touch **Send**). The reply is sent.

5. Deleting Emails

Deleting an email sends it to the Trash folder. To delete emails:

1. Open the Inbox. Refer to *"Reading Email"* on page 39 to learn how.

2. Touch and hold each email that you wish to delete, one at a time. The emails are selected.

3. Touch the 🗑 icon, or touch **Delete**. The Inbox options appear.

4. Touch **Delete**. The selected emails are sent to the Trash folder.

6. Searching the Inbox

To find an email in the Inbox, use the search function, which searches email addresses, message content, and subject lines. To search the Inbox:

1. Open the Inbox. Refer to *"Reading Email"* on page 39 to learn how.

2. Touch the 🔍 icon, or touch **Search** (depending on your device). The virtual keyboard appears.

3. Enter a search word or phrase and touch the 🔍 button (or touch **Search**). The device searches the Inbox and a list of matching results appears.

Managing Applications

Table of Contents

1. Setting Up a Google Account

In order to buy applications, you will need to assign a Google account to your device. To add a Google account:

1. Touch or press the ▦ key. The Home Menu appears.

2. Touch **Settings**. The Settings screen appears.

3. Touch **Accounts**, **Accounts & Sync**, or **Add Account**, depending on your device. The Accounts screen appears. If you touched Add Account, skip to step 5.

4. Touch **Add Account**. The New Account screen appears.

5. Enter your Google Account username and password. If you do not have a Google account, visit **https://accounts.google.com/SignUp?service=mail** from a Web browser on your computer to set one up.

6. You may have to touch **Next** after entering your account information. The Google account is added to your device, and you may now purchase applications.

2. Searching for an Application

You can search for applications in the Play Store,which is the Android application market. There are two ways to search for applications:

Manual Search

To manually search for an application:

1. Touch the ▶️ icon on the Home screen or touch the ⊞ icon and then touch the ▶️ icon. The Play Store opens.

2. Touch the 🔍 icon in the upper right-hand corner of the screen. The virtual keyboard appears.

3. Enter the name of an application or developer and touch the 🔍 button on the keyboard. The matching results appear grouped by media type, such as Games or Productivity.

4. Touch **APPS**. A list of matching application results appears.

5. Touch the name of an application. A description of the application appears.

Browse by Category

To browse applications by category:

1. Touch the ▶️ icon on the Home screen or touch the ⊞ icon and then touch the ▶️ icon. The Play Store opens.

2. Touch **Apps** or **Games**. A list of featured applications appears.

3. Touch the screen and move your finger to the left or right to browse the most popular paid or free applications. Keep swiping your finger to the right to select the Categories tab, where you can browse the application categories.

4. Touch the name of an application. A description of the application appears.

3. Buying an Application

Applications can be purchased directly from your device using the Play Store. To purchase an application from the Play Store:

1. Find an application. Refer to *"Searching for an Application"* on page 43 to learn more.

2. Touch the name of an application. The Application Description screen appears.

3. Follow the instructions below to download the application:

Installing Free Applications

Touch the [INSTALL] button. The Permissions screen appears. Touch the [ACCEPT] button. The application begins to download and the progress is shown. Touch **OPEN** to run the application when it is finished downloading and installing.

Installing Paid Applications

Touch the price of the application. The Permissions screen appears. Touch the [ACCEPT] button. The application begins to download and the progress is shown. You may also need to enter your Google password before the application can be purchased. Touch **OPEN** run the application when it is finished downloading and installing.

Note: When purchasing an application for the first time, Google Checkout asks for your credit card information. The information is saved and used for all subsequent purchases.

4. Uninstalling an Application

Within the first 15 minutes of purchasing an application, it can be uninstalled for a full refund. After 15 minutes have passed, the following instructions only apply to uninstalling an application without receiving a refund. To request a refund and uninstall an application while using the Play Store:

1. Touch the ▣ key, or touch the left edge of the screen and slide your finger to the right while using the Play Store (depending on your device). The Play Store menu appears.

2. Touch **My Apps**. The My Apps screen appears.

3. Touch the application that you wish to remove. The application description appears.

4. Touch **REFUND** if less than 15 minutes have passed. Otherwise, touch **UNINSTALL**. The application is uninstalled and a refund is given if less than 15 minutes have passed.

*Note: If uninstalling without a refund, a confirmation dialog appears after touching Uninstall. Touch **OK**. The application is uninstalled. You can always re-download an application that was purchased and uninstalled for free. Refer to* "Installing a Previously Purchased Application" *on page 46 to learn how to re-download an application.*

5. Adding an Application to Your Wishlist

You may find an application that you like but do not wish to purchase it right away. If you wish to save an application as a favorite, you may add it to your Wishlist. To add an application to your Wishlist:

1. Find an application. Refer to *"Searching for an Application"* on page 43 to learn more.

2. Touch the name of an application. The Application Description screen appears.

3. Touch the ![icon] icon at the top of the screen. The application is added to your Wishlist.

4. Touch the ![key] key, or touch the left edge of the screen and slide your finger to the right while using the Play Store (depending on your device). The Play Store menu appears.

5. Touch **My wishlist**. The Wishlist appears.

6. Installing a Previously Purchased Application

After purchasing an application on an Android device registered to your account, you can download the same application for free on any Android device registered to the same account. To install previously purchased applications while using the Play Store:

1. Touch the ![key] key, or touch the left edge of the screen and slide your finger to the right while using the Play Store (depending on your device). The Play Store menu appears.

2. Touch **My Apps**. The My Apps screen appears.

3. Touch the screen and move your finger to the right. A list of all applications, both installed and uninstalled, appears.

4. Touch the name of an application. The Application description appears.

5. Touch the ![INSTALL] button. The Permissions screen appears.

6. Touch the ![ACCEPT] button. The application is installed on your device.

7. Updating Installed Applications

Application developers will sometimes release updates for their applications. To update your installed applications while using the Play Store:

1. Touch the ▣ key, or touch the left edge of the screen and slide your finger to the right while using the Play Store (depending on your device). The Play Store menu appears.

2. Touch **My Apps**. The My Apps screen appears.

3. Touch an application under 'Updates'. The Application description appears. If there are no applications under 'Updates', then there are no updates available for your installed applications.

4. Touch **UPDATE**. The Permissions screen appears.

5. Touch the ▨ACCEPT button. The application is updated.

Note: You can also touch **UPDATE ALL** *to the right of 'Updates' to update all of your out-of-date applications at once. There is no confirmation dialog when using this method.*

Tips and Tricks

Table of Contents

1. Importing Your Contacts from Another Phone

If you are new to Android, and are coming from another phone, such as an iPhone or a non-smartphone (flip phone), the specialists who sell you the phone (i.e. BestBuy, Radioshack, etc.) will likely offer you the option of transferring all of your contacts. If the specialists are unable to transfer your contacts, the fastest way to add them to your phone is to create a Google account
(here: **https://accounts.google.com/SignUp?service=mail**), and add the contacts' information to your address book.

You will also need to add your newly created Google account to your phone, as described here: *"Setting Up a Google Account"* on page 42. Once your Google account is added, your phone will automatically pull the contacts from your Google address book. Now, every time that you add a new contact to your Google address book, the contact's information will be automatically added to your phone as well.

2. Saving on Data Costs by Connecting to Wi-Fi

When you first buy an Android phone, your service provider will require you to sign up for a data plan. Data allows you to download applications, browse the Web, send and receive email, and much more. The most cost effective strategy is to purchase the smallest, cheapest, data plan, and to connect your phone to your wireless network (Wi-Fi) whenever you are at home or at a coffee shop or airport. To connect to a Wi-Fi network:

1. Touch or press the ▣ key. The Home menu appears.

2. Touch **Settings**. The Settings Screen appears. The instructions for the following steps will vary based on your device.

3. Touch **Wi-Fi** or **Wireless**, depending on your phone. The Wi-Fi or Wireless Settings screen appears. You will need to touch **Wi-Fi** if you see the Wireless Settings screen. Wi-Fi is automatically turned on when you touch **Wi-Fi**.

4. Touch the wireless network to which you would like to connect. The password prompt appears. When your Internet Service Provider set up your network, the provider asked for or indicated the name of your network, as well as the password.

5. Enter your password and touch **Connect**. Your phone connects to your Wi-Fi network, and data will no longer be used. Follow steps 1-3 again, and touch **Wi-Fi** to turn it off. The only time that you should turn Wi-Fi off is in the case of connection loss.

3. Boarding a Plane with Your Phone

Shortly before your plane takes off, your pilot will ask you to turn off all electronics. Before turning off your phone, make sure to turn on Airplane mode, so that you can still safely use it in flight when you turn it back on. To turn on Airplane mode:

1. Touch or press the ▣ key. The Home menu appears.

2. Touch **Settings**. The Settings Screen appears. The instructions for the following steps will vary based on your device.

3. Touch **Wireless**, **More networks**, or **Airplane Mode** (depending on your phone). If you touched Airplane mode, a confirmation dialog appears. Touch **OK** to turn on Airplane mode. Otherwise, the Wireless Networks screen appears.

4. Touch **Airplane Mode** on the Wireless Networks screen. Airplane mode is turned on. Some phones will also allow you to turn on Airplane mode by pressing and holding the power button (as if you were going to turn off the phone).

Note: The procedure for turning on Airplane Mode will vary based on your device.

4. Adjusting the Volume of the Ringer

The ringer on your phone has three settings: sound, vibration, and silent.

Sound

When the Sound is on and you press the volume buttons, the phone makes a sound, which becomes increasingly louder when you press the **Volume Up** button, and quieter when you press the **Volume Down** button.

Vibration

When Vibration is on, the phone will not make any sounds other than alarm sounds. To turn on vibration, press the **Volume Down** button repeatedly until you feel the phone vibrate.

Silent

When Silent mode is on, the phone will not make any sounds, and will not vibrate. Alarm sounds will still be turned on. To turn on Silent mode, press the **Volume Down** one more time after your phone is in Vibration mode. A speaker icon that is crossed out should appear (depending on your phone).

5. Adjusting the Brightness

Since most smartphones today have very large, bright screens, most of your battery is usually drained by the screen itself. To improve your battery life and reduce the strain on your eyes, you may wish to adjust the brightness of your screen. To adjust the brightness:

1. Touch or press the ▭ key. The Home menu appears.

2. Touch **Settings**. The Settings screen appears.

3. Touch **Display**. The Display Settings screen appears. On some phones you will first need to touch **My device** at the top of the screen, while on others, you will be able to touch **Brightness** right away. If you touched **Brightness**, proceed to step 5.

4. Touch **Brightness**. The Brightness window appears. By default, Automatic Brightness is turned on. When Automatic Brightness is on (available on most phones), your phone will automatically lower the brightness of the screen in dark conditions, and raise the brightness in bright conditions.

5. Touch **Automatic brightness**. The ✔ mark next to 'Automatic brightness' disappears and the feature is turned off. An adjustment bar appears.
6. Touch and drag the ◄�○► slider to the left to decrease the brightness, or to the right to increase it. Touch **OK**. The brightness is adjusted. Alternatively, touch **Cancel** to continue using the Automatic Brightness feature.

Note: The procedure for adjusting the brightness will vary based on your device.

6. Turning the Screen Rotation On or Off

When you hold your phone upright and rotate it, the screen will rotate as well (unless you are on the Home screen). This is especially useful when looking at pictures. However, sometimes you may wish to keep the screen from automatically rotating. To turn off Screen Rotation:

1. Touch or press the ▭ key. The Home menu appears.

2. Touch **Settings**. The Settings screen appears.

3. Touch **Display**. The Display Settings screen appears.

4. Touch **Auto-rotate screen** (may vary based on your phone). Automatic screen rotation is turned off. Touch **Auto-rotate screen** again to turn the feature back on.

7. Maximizing Battery Life

There are several things that you can do to increase the battery life of your phone:

- Lock the phone whenever it is not in use. Because of its size and power, leaving the screen turned on will quickly kill the battery. To lock the phone, press the **Power** button once.

- Turn down the brightness or turn on auto-brightness. To learn how to adjust the brightness, refer to *"Adjusting the Brightness"* on page 51.

- Minimize your use of the internet. Using data significantly decreases the battery life.

- Avoid using the camera, and do not use the camera flash, if possible. Both need a lot of battery power to operate.

8. Transferring Documents, Pictures, and Videos to and from Your Computer

You can connect your phone to your computer if you wish to transfer any type of media to and from your computer. To transfer media between your computer and phone:

1. Unplug the charging cable from the charging adapter (the piece that contains the plug). Plug this end into the computer. The USB port on a computer looks like this:  .

2. Plug the other end of the cable into the bottom or side of your phone. Refer to *"Charging the Device"* on page 6 to learn how. Most computers will automatically detect your phone, indicated by a window that appears on your computer screen (unless you are using a Mac). If your computer does not detect the phone, please contact the phone manufacturer to ask what steps you can take.

3. Open **My Computer** (or **Computer** on Windows Vista or later) on a PC and double-click the 'PHONE' portable device, where 'PHONE' refers to the name of your device. On a Mac, open the Android File Transfer program (which you can download here: **http://www.android.com/filetransfer/**). The phone folder opens.

4. Double-click the **Phone** folder, if you are using a PC. The phone folders appear.

5. Double-click a folder. The folder opens.

6. Click and drag a file into the open folder. The file is copied and will appear in the corresponding library. You can also click and drag a file from the Phone folder to your computer.

Troubleshooting

Table of Contents

1. Phone does not turn on

If the phone does not turn on:

- **Recharge the phone** - Use the included wall charger to charge the battery. If the battery power is extremely low, the screen will not turn on for several minutes. Do NOT attempt to use the USB port on your computer to charge the phone, as it will not work.

- **Replace the battery** - If you purchased the phone a long time ago, you may need to replace the battery. Visit your local network provider's store to find out how you can acquire a new battery.

- **Perform a Soft Reset** - If you have done one or both of the above and the phone still does not start, a soft reset should be performed. To perform a soft reset:

1. Take out the battery and wait ten seconds. The phone resets.

2. Re-insert the battery. Press and hold the **Power** button for three seconds. The phone turns on.

2. Phone is not responding

If the phone is frozen or is not responding, try one or more of the following. These steps typically solve most problems on the phone:

- **Restart the phone** - If the phone freezes while running an application, try holding down the **Power** button. If this does not work, the best course of action is to perform a soft reset. Refer to *"Perform a Soft Reset"* above to learn how.

- **Remove Media** - Some downloaded applications or music may freeze up the phone. After restarting the phone, try deleting some of the media. To learn how to delete an application, refer to *"Uninstalling an Application"* on page 45.

3. Can't make a call

If you cannot make a call using the phone, check the following:

- **Service** - If there are no bars shown at the top right of the screen, then the network does not cover you in your location. Try walking to a different location or even to a different part of a building.

- **Airplane Mode** - Make sure Airplane mode is turned off. If it is already off, try turning Airplane mode on for 15 seconds and then turning it back off. Refer to *"Boarding a Plane with Your Phone"* on page 49 to learn how to turn Airplane mode off.

- **Area code** - Make sure you dialed an area code with the phone number.

- **Restart** - Turn the phone off and back on, as this sometimes solves the problem.

4. Can't surf the web

Make sure that you have signal, or that Wi-Fi is is turned on. The signal bars in the upper right-hand corner of the screen indicate whether you have signal. Refer to *"Saving on Data Costs by Connecting to Wi-Fi"* on page 49 to learn more about Wi-Fi.

5. Screen or keyboard does not rotate

If the screen does not turn or the full, horizontal keyboard is not showing when the phone is turned on its side, the problem may be one of the following issues:

- It is very likely that the application does not support the horizontal view.

- Make sure that the phone is not lying flat while rotating. Hold the phone upright to change the orientation in applications that support it.

- Make sure auto-rotate is turned on. Refer to *"Turning the Screen Rotation On or Off"* on page 51 to learn more.

6. Low Microphone Volume, Caller can't hear you

If you are talking to someone who can't hear you, try removing any cases or other accessories, as these may cover up the microphone. If the caller cannot hear you at all, you may have accidentally muted the conversation. To learn how to turn mute on or off while on a call, refer to *"Using the Mute Function During a Voice Call"* on page 16.

If you find yourself accidentally muting the conversation often, there may be something covering up the light sensor, preventing the screen from dimming and locking the mute button. Taking off any accessories may also correct this problem, as some cases cover up the sensor completely.

7. Display does not adjust brightness automatically

If the phone does not dim in dark conditions or does not become brighter in bright conditions, try taking any cases or accessories off. Cases may block the light sensor at the top of the phone, located near the earpiece. Also, Auto Brightness may be turned off. To learn how to turn Auto Brightness on or off, refer to *"Adjusting the Brightness"* on page 51.

8. Application does not install correctly

Sometimes applications may not download or install correctly. If this happens, try canceling the download and re-downloading the application. If the application is already installed, try uninstalling an application and re-installing it. Refer to *"Uninstalling an Application"* on page 45 to learn more.

9. Touchscreen does not respond as expected

If there is a problem with the touchscreen, try the following, in the order in which the steps appear:

1. Remove any cases or screen protectors from the touchscreen.

2. Clean the screen with a soft, damp cloth.

3. Wash and dry your hands thoroughly. Grease and other residue on your skin may cause the touchscreen to function improperly.

4. Restart your device.

10. Phone becomes very hot

Some applications require a lot of power and may cause the phone to become hot to the touch. This is normal and should not affect your device's life span or performance.

11. Camera does not turn on

If the camera does not turn on, try one of the following:

- Make sure the phone's battery is charged and above 15%. The camera will not turn on if the battery level is too low.

- Free up some memory by transferring files to a computer or deleting files from your device, as there may not be enough remaining memory to store new pictures. The camera may not turn on if the memory is too low. Refer to *"Transferring Documents, Pictures, and Videos to and from Your Computer"* on page 52 to learn how to transfer files to your computer. Refer to *"Uninstalling an Application"* on page 45 to learn how to remove applications from your phone.

- Restart the phone and try turning on the camera again.

Index

,

DISCARD

Made in the USA
Lexington, KY
06 October 2016